THE SECRET TO BEING RICH

IT WILL BRING YOU A WEALTH

Written by Niyazi Şahin

ALL MONEYMAKERS HAVE A SECRET THEY
DON'T EVEN KNOW THEY HAVE AND IT
WILL BE VERY EASY FOR YOU TO GET RICH
WHEN YOU FIND IT OUT.

WRITER'S NOTE:

I don't promise to show you how to make money without working or tell you which work is the most lucrative one in this book. Maybe I won't make you rich quickly and I won't even send you money. What I will do in this book is just try to explain what money-hunters should do in the right order. I will tell you what the main thing we need to do is, as difficult as it may seem, and show you how to do it. It won't be so easy but will get easier as you understand it.

Every man is the architect of his own fortune.

Sallust

SECRETS TO BEING RICH

WANT AND DREAM

To want and to dream are actually the first two steps those who want to be rich should take. It's so difficult to achieve something without dreaming of it. Imagination is what actually makes us think of the things we want to happen. It paves the way to success; it shows how much you want to succeed; it helps us make future plans; it determines our future.

When we want to do something, we first dream of it. In other words, we build it up in our mind. It's too hard to want something we don't imagine.

Now here comes the question: Are we sure we imagine things in the best way?

Imagining something means you ask life, God, universe or whatever you believe in for it. It's the easiest way of wanting something.

People tend to limit their imagination with their current conditions but there's actually no limit for dreams. You have the power to imagine. So, it's wrong to restrict it. Those who dream of getting rich probably have a certain amount of money in their mind. Why limit our imagination when asking an infinite being for something? Let's dream of something unreachable and believe wholeheartedly that we'll get it one day. I know it doesn't sound very convincing at first but you should always believe in it. Many rich people have run after their dreams, perhaps spending many nights dreaming instead of going to sleep, they have made an effort for their dreams to come true and eventually they succeeded. Here you are the first secret to being rich: Dream. To dream is to plan your future. It's the first step towards being rich.

Now take the limits off and start dreaming of your future and wealth; and strengthen your dreams by supporting them with your plans.

The greatest works have been accomplished by
people with big dreams.

William Russell

I owe my achievements to my dreams in my youth.

Napoléon Bonaparte

The greatest achievement was at first and for a time
a dream. The oak sleeps in the acorn; the bird waits
in the egg; and in the highest vision of the soul a
waking angel stirs. Dreams are the seedlings of
reality.

James Allen

Stop praying without acting! If you want a tree, then sow a seed.

Rumi

TRUST YOURSELF

I think that getting rich would not change so many things in the lives of those who don't trust themselves. Indeed, I believe they won't even be able to get rich. Please always bear in mind that people won't trust those who doesn't trust themselves and even buy the product made by them.

This chapter of the book is very important in this regard. If you don't trust yourself or believe you aren't able to achieve something, I think you should stop reading this book because otherwise it won't help you anyway and will end up being an ordinary book.

If you're still reading, it means you have a trust in yourself and that's quite good news! Just remember that only those who trust themselves will achieve success in life and get rich. Trusting yourself is not only about yourself, but also helps you trust the product you made as much as you trust yourself. So, we can say those who trust themselves or the their products deserve success and wealth. If you don't believe in the product you made, invented or developed, you can't make others believe in it. Without believing, we can't market any product or even ourselves. Only if you trust yourself will the importance of your work will become clear. When you look at rich people, you'll see that they're very self-confident. They aren't self-confident as they are rich; actually, they're rich as they are self-confident. Since they believe and trust themselves, people value them or their products, making them rich. Getting rich is not based only on your effort, you also need the influence your work has on people. Whether others prefer you or your products depends on your trust in yourself or the product you make. That's why you should trust yourself. If you don't trust yourself, you can read books about it or receive a therapy. I regret to tell you that, unless you trust yourself, you shouldn't dream of getting rich because, you'll never be a rich person ☹

Unless you trust yourself, you'll probably spend your years trying to make a boss, a self-confident one, even richer. Unless you trust yourself, you won't even be able to take risks, so you will strive for others and envy their lives. People who don't trust themselves are not even able to dream. Even when they dream of something, they can't think without limits. They always restrict themselves and can't overcome their "can't-do" attitude. They can actually do it but it always depends on whether they dream freely and trust themselves. You should always respect and love yourself and be sure that you can achieve success. Unless you trust yourself, you don't need to try to make people trust you or get rich. Now I'm going to reveal another secret to being a self-respecting, self-loving and self-confident person.

When you believe, your mind will find way to do.

David J. Schwartz

The first and greatest victory is to conquer yourself.

Platon

Self-confidence is the first requisite to great
undertakings.

Samuel Johnson

FOCUS

The next step following dreaming and trusting ourselves is focusing on what we do. We should focus on our work just like a student preparing for a university exam or a competitor preparing for a contest.

Focusing doesn't mean thinking intensely only, it also includes researching and examining the thing that we will do and focusing on what can be done to improve it. It might take hours, days or maybe years but I think people who trust themselves and dream of achieving success can focus on their work and succeed. You need to go beyond just thinking about your goal and do experiments and researches, and prepare data about it. If your goal is a product, you need to focus on developing it to make it better, cheaper, newer, more aesthetical or more featured.

When you trust your product or whatever you make, the question you should focus on is this:

Why should people prefer it?

Ask this question to yourself constantly. Then prepare a minimum of ten answers. If those answers satisfy you, it means you're on the right track.

The more you focus on right things, the faster you'll achieve your goal, believe you me! You can see it clearly when you look at the lives of rich people: They focus on a product or a work deeply, sacrificing their time and even their youth.

They dream of success, believe in and trust themselves, focus on their goal and never give up. And at the end, they make their dreams come true.

Perhaps we must make a basic choice as to whether
we will live in fear or focus on what we want.

John Izzo

Don't focus on the what ifs. Focus on what is.

Vi Keeland

Choosing the right path in life requires constant
focus, courage and discipline.

Gregory Bassham

TAKE ACTION

Tomorrow you'll be brave, you say? Fool! Dive today.

Rumi

Rumi actually put it very clearly. Many people have always dreamt of success, trusted in themselves, made plans but never took action. They always postponed it and never became successful.

This is the most crucial part of this book. It's actually your first step towards what you'll do. Though it's the hardest part, it becomes the easiest and best part after you make the first step.

Taking action is like a preliminary contract for something to happen, or sowing the seeds of a tree. You've had dreams of success, supported them with your plans, had a complete trust in yourself, focused on your goal and brought out something. The only thing you'll need to do is take action because you will never achieve success without taking action, which makes this part the hardest one. That's because you might need to sacrifice your life. Some will quit their job and some others will have to leave their city. They might have made plans for future but it's very difficult to achieve it.

I suggest that you do it right now. You can do it when you feel ready. Don't hesitate to act even if you feel ready at night. There is no harm in staying awake for just one night but postponing your dreams can make you regret so much in future. You might think you have good reasons to postpone them, but remember that every day you don't take action puts back the day you'll become a rich person. You should stop making up excuses not to act. Don't forget that there's no guarantee of tomorrow.

Now it's your turn! The only obstacle between you and your goal is you. When you follow these steps in the right order, I mean, dream of success, trust yourself, focus on what you need to do and take the action required for your goal, you'll find your fortune in any case.

Now you have the secret. It's free of charge and can be tried any time you like.

If there's a business or invention you have long been dreaming of, start working for it right now. Your fortune will find you one day as long as you follow the steps in the order I prescribed and keep my tips in your mind. Believe in it!

History has witnessed so many people who used this secret, knowingly or unknowingly, and their fortune found them at some point in their lives.

Do you wonder who they are? Here you are the answer:

Bill Gates,

Elon Musk,

Jeff Bezos,

Steve Jobs,

Mark Zuckerberg

and hundreds of other names... I don't know whether they knew this secret or not but it found them because they made all the required steps in the right order. There is no difference between you and them. You are someone living in this world just like them. The only difference was money but now that you know the secret, it's of no importance. Now it's your turn. I think you should take an action as soon as possible to close the gap.

Good luck!

There is a good life waiting for you. It's just waiting for you to grab it.

Robert Kiyosaki

www.ingramcontent.com/pod-product-compliance
Lightning Source LLC
Chambersburg PA
CBHW070242260726
48658CB00006BA/2396